My Life with Autism

written by **Mari Schuh** • art by **Isabel Muñoz**

AMICUS ILLUSTRATED and AMICUS INK

are published by Amicus
P.O. Box 1329, Mankato, MN 56002
www.amicuspublishing.us

Editor: Gillia Olson
Designer: Kathleen Petelinsek

Library of Congress Cataloging-in-Publication Data
Names: Schuh, Mari C., 1975- author. | Muñoz, Isabel, illustrator.
Title: My life with autism / Mari Schuh ; illustrated by Isabel Muñoz.
Description: Mankato, Minnesota : Amicus, [2021] | Series: My life with... | Includes bibliographical references. | Audience: Ages 6-9
| Audience: Grades 2-3 | Summary: "Meet Zen! He loves to draw and play video games. He also has autism. Zen is real and so are his
experiences. Learn about his life in this illustrated narrative nonfiction picture book for elementary students"—Provided by
publisher. Identifiers: LCCN 2019048111 (print) | LCCN 2019048112 (ebook) | ISBN 9781681519920 (library
binding) | ISBN 9781681526393 (paperback) | ISBN 9781645490777 (pdf)
Subjects: LCSH: Autism in children—Juvenile literature. | Autistic children—United States—Biography—Juvenile literature.
Classification: LCC RJ506.A9 S419 2021 (print) | LCC RJ506.A9 (ebook) | DDC 618.92/85882—dc23
LC record available at https://lccn.loc.gov/2019048111
LC ebook record available at https://lccn.loc.gov/2019048112

For Zen and his family -MS

About the Author

Mari Schuh's love of reading began with cereal boxes at
the kitchen table. Today, she is the author of hundreds of
nonfiction books for beginning readers. With each book, Mari
hopes she's helping kids learn a little bit more about the world
around them. Find out more about her at marischuh.com.

About the Illustrator

To paint for a living was Isabel Muñoz' dream, and now she's
proud to be the illustrator of several children books. Isabel
works from a studio based in a tiny, cloudy, green and lovely
town in the north of Spain. You can follow her at isabelmg.com.

Hi! My name is Zen. I'm a kid, just like you. We might enjoy the same things. I like to draw and play video games. We might have differences, too. I have autism. Let me tell you about my life!

Kids who have autism are born with it. Doctors aren't sure what causes it. You can't tell if someone has autism just by looking at them.

Autism affects how a person acts, feels, and talks. It affects each person a little differently. People call it the autism spectrum. That means each person with autism has their own talents and needs.

You might see kids with autism repeat movements.
Some kids might spin or rock back and forth.
They might flap their arms or kick.

When I was younger, I walked on my toes and made clicking sounds with my tongue. A therapist taught me how to stop.

Talking and knowing how to act is hard for kids with autism. Some kids with autism talk just a little or not at all. We often don't get jokes. I repeat words and I avoid looking at people. I might talk loudly or stand too close. Sometimes, people stare at me.

New foods bother me. I eat only warm foods and I drink only one kind of juice. People with autism tend to eat only their favorites.

Kids with autism can be sensitive to light and sound. Loud sounds and big crowds bother me. We go home when it gets too loud.

Being sensitive to touch is common, too. I like to wear soft shirts without tags or scratchy seams. My favorite blanket and pillow are super soft.

I like routines and so do lots of other kids with autism. We get upset when things change. When I travel, I need to bring my juice, snacks, blanket, and pillow. After a worker cleaned our hotel room, I couldn't find my pillow! It was in a closet with a new pillowcase on it. I put my old, soft pillowcase back on.

Mom and dad make sure I don't get bored when I travel. I have so much fun!

Like everyone, kids with autism have their own talents. I'm good with computers. I can find lots of facts in only a few minutes!

My class at school is small. A teacher's helper is with me all day. She helps me learn. I join other classes for art, gym, and band. But I don't feel like I belong. All the kids know one another.

It can be hard for kids with autism to make friends. I have been invited to only one birthday party. I ask kids to play with me, but they don't want to. So, I play alone.

I'm happy that I joined a science club after school. The kids there made sure I wasn't left out. We worked as a team. They listened to my ideas. It was great!

Guess what? I finally got invited to play at someone's house! I didn't get the jokes the kids were telling. But I had fun and so did they. I think I'll have lots of friends when I grow up.

Meet Zen

Hi! I'm Zen. I live on Long Island, New York, with my dad, mom, brother, and sister. I'm the youngest. I love playing games on my computer and playing with my dog, Buddy. I am smart, honest, and kind. When people are sad, I try to make them smile. My favorite class is art class and my favorite color is blue. I'm proud of who I am and what I have learned.

Respecting People with Autism

Treat a person with autism like you would any person. Be friendly, kind, and understanding. Don't tease or bully them.

When you meet someone with autism, be friendly and say hi. Don't ignore them or walk away.

Be calm and nice when spending time with someone with autism. Try not to get frustrated or yell.

Everyone likes to be part of a group. Be sure to invite kids with autism to play and go to birthday parties. They want to have fun, just like other kids.

If a kid with autism is talking loudly, don't stare, laugh, or point at them. Just listen to what they are saying.

No two people in the world are exactly the same. Each person has things they are good at and things that they like to do. This is also true for people with autism.

Helpful Terms

autism spectrum The wide number of ways that autism affects how a person talks, feels, and acts. Autism is a condition of the brain. People with autism have a hard time making friends and getting to know other people. The spectrum means autism affects each person differently.

routine A regular way or pattern of doing things that is the same each time.

sensitive Easily hurt or affected by small changes or differences.

talent Something a person is good at doing.

therapist A person who is trained to help people with conditions, disorders, and illnesses learn new skills.

Read More

Duling, Kaitlyn. **My Friend Has Autism**. All Kinds of Friends. Minneapolis: Jump!, Inc., 2019.

Levine, Michelle. **Autism**. Living with... Mankato, Minn.: Amicus High Interest, 2015.

Spilsbury, Louise. **Questions and Feelings About Autism**. Questions and Feelings About... North Mankato, Minn.: Picture Window Books, a Capstone Imprint, 2019.

Websites

KIDSHEALTH: AUTISM SPECTRUM DISORDER

https://kidshealth.org/en/kids/autism.html

Read this website to learn more about people who have autism.

KIDS' QUEST: AUTISM

https://www.cdc.gov/ncbddd/kids/autism.html

This website is full of helpful information about autism.

SESAME STREET AND AUTISM

http://autism.sesamestreet.org

Find helpful information about autism.

Every effort has been made to ensure that these websites are appropriate for children. However, because of the nature of the Internet, it is impossible to guarantee that these sites will remain active indefinitely or that their contents will not be altered.